Edwin W. Jackson

Ward-Jackson's Gymnastics for the Fingers and Wrist

being a system of gymnastics, based on anatomical principles, for

developing and strengthening the muscles of the hand for musical,

mechanical, and medical purposes

Edwin W. Jackson

Ward-Jackson's Gymnastics for the Fingers and Wrist
being a system of gymnastics, based on anatomical principles, for developing and strengthening the muscles of the hand for musical, mechanical, and medical purposes

ISBN/EAN: 9783337885915

Printed in Europe, USA, Canada, Australia, Japan

Cover: Foto ©Andreas Hilbeck / pixelio.de

More available books at **www.hansebooks.com**

WARD-JACKSON'S

GYMNASTICS

FOR

THE FINGERS AND WRIST;

BEING

A SYSTEM OF GYMNASTICS,

BASED ON ANATOMICAL PRINCIPLES,— FOR DEVELOPING
AND STRENGTHENING THE MUSCLES OF THE HAND; FOR
MUSICAL, MECHANICAL, AND MEDICAL PURPOSES.

BY

E. WARD-JACKSON, J.P.

With Thirty-five Diagrams.

NEW YORK:

G. SCHIRMER.

35 UNION SQUARE.

CONTENTS.

IV CONTENTS.

CONTENTS.

IV

CONTENTS.

INTRODUCTORY REMARKS

ON THE ORIGIN OF THIS SYSTEM OF GYMNASTICS FOR THE FINGERS AND WRIST.

THE subject of this little work develops, on anatomical and physiological principles, a system of Gymnastics for the Fingers and Wrist, the object of which is—to lay a solid and scientific foundation for the acquisition of technical skill in the fingers and wrist, as applied to the playing on musical instruments and to finger work generally.

I may simply state, that both the scientific principles and the practical utility of this system of Gymnastics have met with the approval of the highest anatomical, musical, and gymnastic authorities of Germany; at whose special solicitation I was induced to make these discoveries known by means of public and private lectures, *delivered gratis in the German language in many German cities*, during the summer of 1864.

And I have also the satisfaction of knowing that this little work has met with the same approval from the medical, musical, and gymnastic authorities in this country, and been a means of practical utility among those for whom it is more particularly intended.

In all the gymnastic establishments throughout Europe and the civilized world gymnastic exercises have been introduced for every part of the body *except for the Fingers*, notwithstanding that it is these important members of the human frame--with the mental organs—which chiefly distinguish man from the brute creation.

If any one should desire to know in what manner I, as a private individual, came to hit upon these discoveries, I answer simply:—

When I was twelve or thirteen years of age I learnt the violin, and afterwards, for upwards of thirty-five years, discontinued it. But, later in life, desiring to accompany my children, I was induced to take it up again. I then found that, although I was in all other respects exceedingly strong and healthy, and capable of all athletic exercises, my fingers and hands in a few minutes became painfully fatigued; in fact, I found that my *fingers* were the only weak parts of my body. This happened a few years ago, exciting in me great surprise and an earnest desire to search into the cause. I thought to myself, "There must underlie some unknown hidden cause to account for this phenomenon. I will thoroughly probe the matter." For this purpose I then put myself in the way of those individually who earned their bread by the sweat of their brow—viz., the smith, the joiner, the bricklayer, the labourer, the peasant, the gardener, the wood-cutter, the miner, &c., &c. I found that all these persons worked with their *arms*, and thereby acquired muscle like

steel and arms like giants; but that none of them
worked with their *fingers*.

After this I visited boys' and girls' schools, and
also obs?rved them in their families; and there I
found again that nearly all of them in their work
made *no use* of the fingers. The same observation
I made with the educated classes, of every age
and sex.

This discovered to me the fact that the muscles
of the fingers are *extremely little exercised* in the
ordinary occupations of life; and must, therefore,
on physiological grounds be weak—a fact of much
importance.

I then repaired to the *most renowned gymnastic*
establishments of the Continent, and begged to be
shown all the varied gymnastic exercises practised
on the body, from the crown of the head to the sole
of the foot; and when all these various movements
had been exhibited before me, I inquired, "But
where are your gymnastic exercises for the *fingers?*"
"We have none; we never thought of it." "But they
require them surely as much, or more, than all!"
"It has never occurred to us; we did not know the
fingers required gymnastics, and they have been
entirely overlooked."

I thereupon visited houses and institutions where
men *do* work with their fingers—viz., where carvers
in wood and ivory, in steel, copper, and stone,
painters and draughtsmen, watchmakers and fine
mechanists, spinners and weavers, printers and
compositors, &c, drive their trade ; and after that,

people who are in the habit of writing much, and even the whole day, such as authors, copyists, clerks, stenographers, lithographers, as well as sempstresses and workwomen;—in short, all those who have much finger-work, or earn their living by their fingers. And here I observed all kinds of *finger diseases*, such as stiffness of the joints and limbs, writers' cramp, hands and forearms debilitated in the highest degree, paralyzed limbs, nervous weakness, &c. Then I said to myself, "A light begins to dawn upon me. I find, *first*, that the fingers are the least exercised, in the ordinary occupations of life, of all the active members of the body; *secondly*, that they are on that account relatively and physiologically the weakest; and *thirdly*, that they are also the *only* active members which are not gymnastically trained and treated. I must consider the matter now ANATOMICALLY, PHYSIOLOGICALLY, and GYMNASTICALLY."

And I forthwith began to make all sorts of experiments, for the purpose of gymnastically exercising, stretching, and developing the muscles, the ligaments, and joints of the fingers and hands in all directions, so as to strengthen and prepare them for playing the piano and the violin, as well as other instruments, and for all kinds of finger-work and handicraft.

In doing so I studied the physiology of the muscles and ligaments, and directed especial attention to the *transverse metacarpal ligament.* In comparing this anatomy with the difficulties experienced, I sought to discover a means more particularly of stretching the *ligaments* or bands which run *transversely* across the hands and knuckles. This I succeeded in effecting; and then I discovered, to my astonishment, that the moment I had applied my gymnastic movements to these stout and very obstinate elastic bands, the *muscles* became instantaneously looser, and moved with greatly increased freedom and agility. In a word, the *muscles were set free.*

Then I said to myself, "I now see as clear as sunlight whence arise the extraordinary difficulties of learning to play the piano and violin. They arise from the very fact that an art the most difficult, from a muscular point of view, which we know of, has to be performed with the *least practised* and proportionately, the *weakest of muscles.* The impediments and difficulties in almost all cases can be referred to the muscles; and it is this weakness which must be overcome."

Upon this I repaired to anatomical, chirurgical, and medical institutions, in order to study still further the anatomy of the hand, the fingers, and the arm. I found that the muscles, the ligaments, and the tendons of the fingers and hands consist of elastic masses, intersecting the hand; and I especially discovered, after a number of experiments, that the TRANSVERSE LIGAMENTS, *unless they be exercised, remain quiet and stiff, and impede to a certain extent the movements and activity of the muscles,* when the latter are more than ordinarily exerted; t at in order practically to exercise and stretch

them, and particularly the TRANSVERSE ligaments
and tendons, and to render them strong and supple,
it is necessary not only to move the fingers up and
down, but laterally also; that, in short, both
muscles and ligaments ought to be practised gymnastically; and that the *fatigue* and the *danger to
health*, the *nervous weakness*, and the *disgust* often
observed in musical students arise from the *following
causes:*—

Firstly, that the muscles, tendons, and ligaments
of the hand and fingers are proportionately the least
practised, and, consequently, as stated before, the
weakest;

Secondly, that they have *never* been **gymnastically**
trained or treated;

Thirdly, that the methods now in use for
strengthening those weak muscles, and rendering
them flexible, are insufficient and erroneous;

Fourthly, that the *transverse ligaments have
never been stretched*; thus, on these several
grounds, hampering the learning of music with
unnatural difficulties, and with exertions of the
muscular and nervous system injurious to health;

Fifthly, that so soon as the muscles are properly
and gymnastically exercised, and the ligaments and
tendons stretched, the fingers, set at liberty, move
glibly and freely over the instrument, on the simplest anatomical and physiological grounds.

The idea had taken hold of me that a hiatus and
a want in the method of learning and practising
music, also in finger-work of various kinds, existed,

and I set to work to fill up the former and to satisfy the latter. The exposition of this method having met with cordial approval, I now offer the result of my labours, in a new and cheap edition, to artists, musical students, and to all friends of music, as well as to all those who work much with their fingers, or who suffer from finger disease; also to anatomists, physiologists, surgeons, and gymnasts; indulging the hope that, if applied correctly and carefully, they will go far towards removing the evils to which I have alluded, and be of much practical usefulness and advantage.

E. WARD-JACKSON, J.P.

Weston-super-Mare, 1873.

CHAPTER I.

ANATOMY OF THE HAND.—ON LIGAMENTS,
TENDONS, ETC. ETC

As regards the system of the gymnastic training
of the fingers in particular, which I am now placing
before the public, it is founded on an important
fact, namely, the action of the LIGAMENTS AND
TENDONS.

It has been acknowledged at all times that
the ligaments and tendons play, in these exercises,
an indispensable part, and it has hitherto never
been sufficiently acknowledged or explained. It
is further known, that the principal method *now in
use* of strengthening and rendering flexible the
joints and muscles of the fingers in playing the
piano, consists in alternately raising and drop-
ping the fingers, and that this method requires
very great exertion, and consumes very much
time. Now, I have found, by means of many
different experiments and exercises, which I
have made with the hand and the fingers, that
the tight ligaments and skin-folds intersecting
the hand *transversely,** unless they be properly

* Joseph Hyrtl: Lehrbuch der Anatomie. 4te Auflage. Wien, 1855.
Erasmus Wilson, F. R. S.: System of Human Anatomy. 4th Edition.
London, 1862.

exercised, remain firm and stiff, and, for this very reason, *impede the movements of the muscles* whenever they are more than ordinarily exerted; while, on the contrary, the stretching of the *transversal ligaments* produces a remarkable influence on the movability of the fingers and the hand, facilitates the work of the *muscles*, and imparts to them freedom, steadiness, and precision.

This result can only be explained by the fact that the ligaments and folds of the hand, having been stretched by the cork cylinders, have become loosened, and, therefore, as I said before, let loose the muscles in their fatiguing work. If, on the other hand, all the muscles, ligaments, and tendons are put into motion in both directions, longitudinally and transversely, they soon become strong and flexible.

CHAPTER II.

THE MUSCLES OF THE HAND AND OF THE FINGERS.

LEAVING aside the vessels and nerves uncon-
nected with our subject, we may describe the
hand as being composed of three classes of
organs: 1. Bones with joints; 2. Ligaments; 3.
Muscles.

1. BONES WITH JOINTS.

The hand is subdivided into five separate
limbs (fingers), lying one at the side of the
other, and being, at the lower end, firmly joined
together into one whole. Each of these five
limbs (fingers) is composed of a row of bones,
having the nature of long bones. The first of
these bones, next to the lower arm, is called
the metacarpal or middle-hand bone (Fig. 1 *a*);
the others are called finger-joints. The thumb
has only two finger-joints, the other fingers three
each. The *fourth and fifth fingers are the
weakest of all.*

The union of the five fingers into one whole
is effected by means of the extremities of the
middle-hand bones, commonly known as knuckles
which are turned towards the forearm, being connected with one another by *very tight transversa*

Fig. 1.

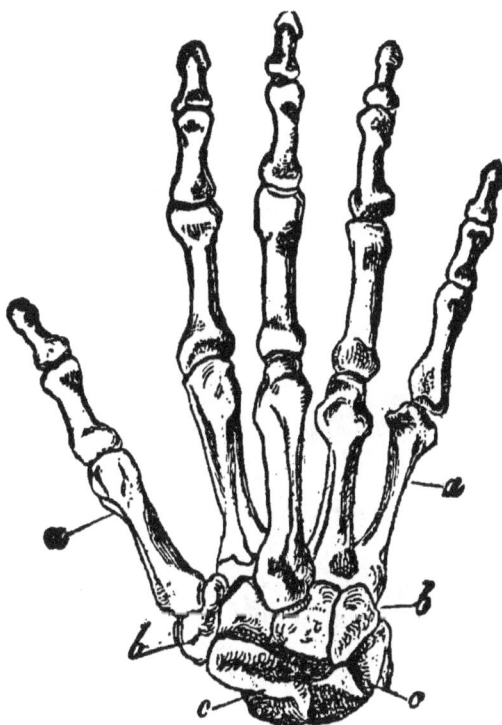

ligaments (Fig. 2 *aa* and Fig. 3 *bb*), and being thus
connected, are again fixed to a row of four roundish
bones, joined to one another in the same manner
(Fig. 1 *b*). Thus, the five middle-hand bones and
the four bones of the upper wrist form one firm
structure. In this structure the middle-hand bone
of the thumb and of the little finger can be more
easily moved than the others.

On account of this movability of the two extreme middle-hand bones, it is possible to move

Fig. 2.

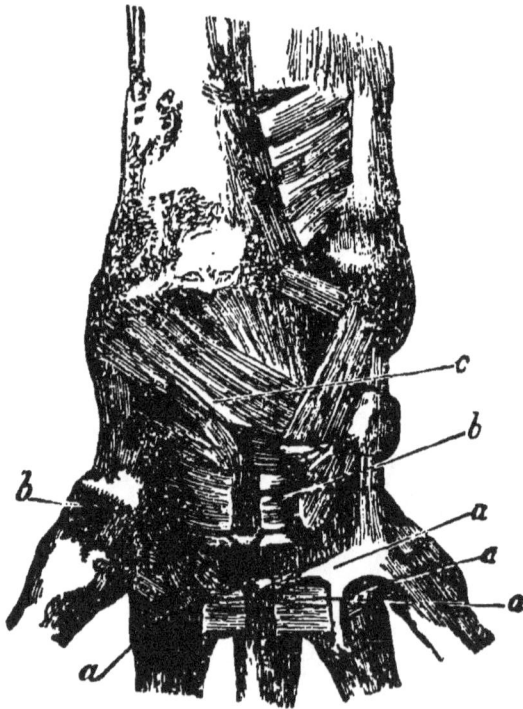

the two edges of the hand close to one another, whereby the cavity of the hand assumes the shape of a groove.

The structure here described (the hand, in the narrower sense of the word) is joined to the lower arm by a row of three muscles (the posterior row of the bones of the wrist, Fig. 1 c). The movement between these bones and the hand is hardly anything but a hinge movement ; that between them and the lower arm, however, is a movement in almost all directions. The bending and stretch-ing of the hand is, therefore, produced with the participation of both joints, the side movement of the hand, however, almost exclusively by the joint situated between the posterior row of the bones of the wrist and the lower arm.*

2. LIGAMENTS.

All the finger joints are provided with capsules, which are woven out of strong *transversal* fibres (Fig. 3 *aa*). The bones of the wrist are connected between themselves and with the bones of the middle-hand by tight transversal and longitudinal ligaments, as seen in Fig. 2 *aa*, *bb*. Lastly, the *two ends of the middle-hand bones, or knuckles, are connected with one another and with the first joints of the fingers by a separate, strong, trans-versal ligament* (Fig. 2 *aa*, 3 *bb*).

3. THE MUSCLES OF THE HAND consist

1. Of muscles (four in number) rising from the lower arm and bending the wrist up and down, right and left (Fig. 3 *c*, *d*, *e*).

2. Of muscles of the fingers, these are sub-divided into —

a. Extensors of the fingers, being situated in the back part of the hand and rising from the bones of the lower arm (Fig. 4 *a*).

b. Benders of the fingers. Two muscles, the one for the second joints of the fingers (Fig. 3 *d*),

---

* Luther Holden, Manual of Anatomy (London, 1861), Lecturer on Anatomy in Bartholomew's Hospital. Hermann Meyer, Lehrbuch der Physiologischen Anatomie. Leipzig, 1856.

Fig. 8.

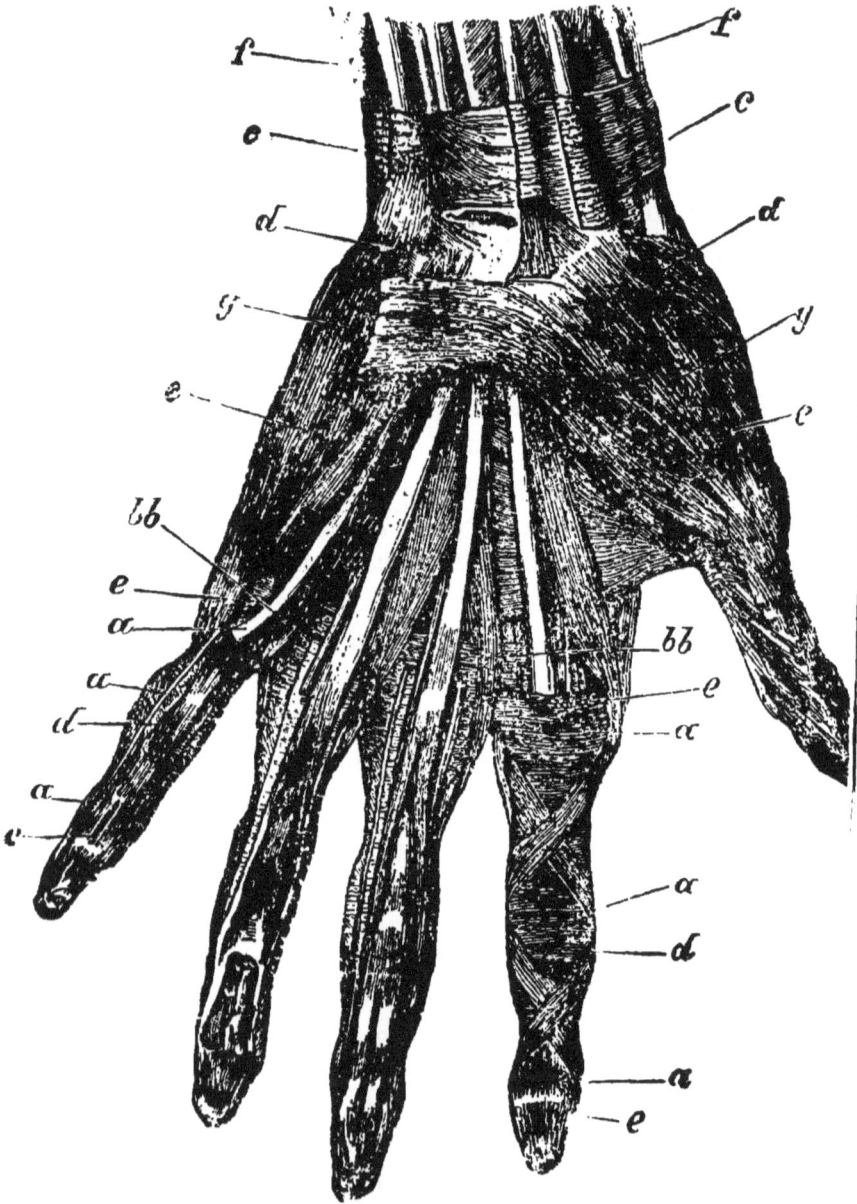

the other for the first joints of the fingers and
the joints of the nails (Fig. 3 *e*) also rising from
the bones of the lower arm.

c. Contractors of the fingers, rising from the
hand itself, between the bones of the middle-hand
(Fig. 4 *b*), and extending as far as the first finger-
joint (Fig. 4 *b*).

d. Two muscles, also rising from the cavity of
the hand, and moving the little finger towards the
thumb (Fig. 3 *g*).

Lumbricales, or Flexores primi Internodii Digi-
torium, are situated in the hollow of the hand,
and pass to their tendinous implantations with the
interossei at the first joint of each finger, externally
and laterally, next the thumb (Fig. 4 *a*, *b*). These
perform those minute motions of the fingers when
the second and third internodes are curvated by
the muscles, and therefore are used in playing
musical instruments, whence they are named Musculi Fidicinales, or fiddle-muscles *

* William Cowper, Myotomia reformata. London 1724. Richard
Quain, Professor of Clinical Surgery, Surgeon-Extraordinary to the
Queen.

B 2

CHAPTER III.

EFFECTS OF THIS GYMNASTIC TREATMENT ON THE MUSCLES, LIGAMENTS, AND JOINTS OF THE FINGERS AND THE HAND. *

AFTER the explanation just given, it may readily be conceived what effects the cork cylinders placed between the fingers, and the gymnastic staff must produce on the joints and ligaments of the hand.

1. The ligaments connecting the bones of the middle-hand amongst themselves and with the fingers (Fig. 2 *aa*) are extended and stretched (Fig. 3 *bb*), and thus those joints, so important in playing on musical instruments, are rendered more movable.

2. The connecting links between the bones of the middle-hand and the bones of the wrist are loosened (Fig. 2 *bb*).

3. Almost all the ligaments of the cavity of the hand are made flexible.

4. At the same time, all the muscles of the hand, and particularly the muscles situated between the bones (Fig. 4 *b*), generally so little practised, are

---

* Anatomists and physicians of great eminence have observed to me, "Your anatomical researches have solved some important questions long held in dispute by physiologists, and are of great practical value."

Fig. 4.

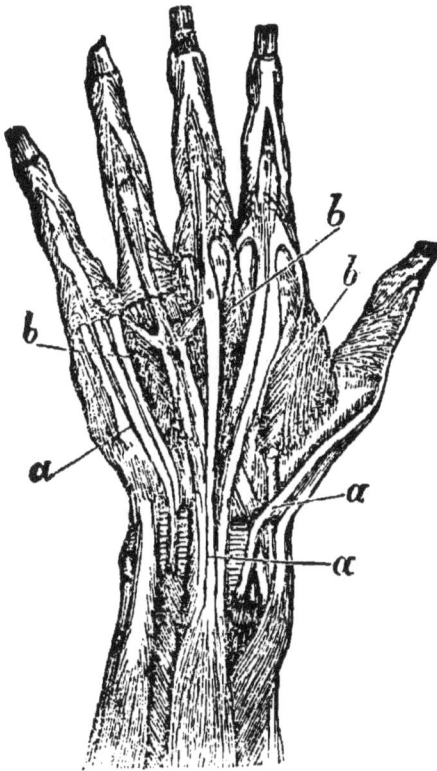

stirred into activity by the cork cylinders, the staff, and the free exercises.

From the diagrams (Figs. 2 and 3) it may be plainly seen, what was mentioned before, viz., that the movement of the middle-hand and of the bones of the wrist in general, unless specially practised, is very inconsiderable; while, through the cork cylinder gymnastics prescribed in this work, that limited movement of the bones is rendered more

easy. It may also be seen from the diagrams, that
if both the great and the small *tight transversal
ligaments* remain still and firm, they impede and
render more difficult the free movement of the
fingers in every direction; and these ligaments will
always remain stiff and tight unless they be
specially trained.

For this reason the cork cylinder exercise, just
mentioned, is particularly intended to loosen the
impeding *transversal ligaments*, as well as to
exercise and strengthen all the muscles of the hand
and fingers.

To convince yourself that this opinion is correct,
extend your fingers for two minutes only with the
cylinders alluded to, and you will find that the
fingers instantaneously move much more easily,
and that the muscles, liberated from their tight,
stiff neighbours, act with much greater freedom.

In the same manner as with the cylinders, the
greatest advantage may be experienced from the
use of the gymnastic staff or stick.

The principle on which these movements **are**
founded is, that by them almost all the muscles
of the hand and the fingers — the smallest
as well as the largest, which, in playing musical
instruments and all the other occupations of the
fingers, bear the chief part — are stirred into
action. At the same time the extraordinary
effect of the free exercises on the large finger-
joints and on the ligaments and tendons is increased.
And further, every portion of the hand and

fingers, ligaments, tendons, joints, and particularly
the muscles, are well practised, strengthened, and
rendered flexible, by the fingers being stretched and
extended on, pressed and exercised against a solid
body. Finally, while imparting to the muscles of
the fingers and hand far greater strength and ease
than the continued quick movement on the musical
instrument is calculated to effect, all these exercises
affect the *nerves* in a lesser degree, and prepare
the fingers for all kinds of work.

These results, observed and tested by me countless
times, are of the greatest importance to all those
who work with their fingers, but more particularly
to those engaged in musical pursuits; who, instead
of being overwhelmed with fatiguing work as before,
will find that by these exercises their studies are
facilitated and divested of much of their previous
trouble and vexation.

THE WRIST.

This joint, which for players on the piano and
other instruments is of such great importance
(Fig. 2 *c*), should also be exercised gymnastically;
since by means of the gymnastic exercises here
recommended, strength and flexibility will be gained
in a very short time, and a great deal of trouble
saved. Nor ought it to be overlooked that, for all
those who so work with their fingers, a flexible,
pliant wrist is a great help, and that by it all
joints of the hand are made to act harmoniously
together.

CHAPTER IV.

NEGLECT HITHERTO OF THE HAND AND FINGERS.

MANY books have been written on gymnastics, but I am not acquainted with one which treats of the gymnastical exercise of the *fingers*. Why these important members of the human body should, until now, have been so much overlooked and neglected, it is difficult to understand. For, as Professor Richter of Dresden says, "Next to the more powerful development of the brain, it is almost exclusively the structure and skill of the fingers and hand which raises man above the brute, and has made him ruler of the earth."

In order therefore, to heighten the capacities of the human hand, the joints of the hand and fingers should, from early youth, be exercised gymnastically, as much and in as many various ways as possible, partly by free exercises, partly by means of mechanical appliances.

Gymnastics, according to anatomists and physicians, is the *stretching*, *extending*, *pressing*, and *training* of the muscles, the ligaments, and the limbs of the body.*

---

* The following quotations from the works of some of the leading authorities may be of interest to the reader: —

"Methodical gymnastic exercises of the hand and fingers afford the

Flexibility, agility, and strength can be acquired only by means of a regular exercise of the muscles of the body.

Strength and power impart agility and quickness. This every physician and every sensible man knows.

A soldier only becomes fit for his work after the muscles of his body have been gymnastically attended to and developed. Any man, having to perform hard physical labour, must exercise his muscles gymnastically, and every one ought to exercise those particular limbs the use of which is most necessary for his profession.

And more than anyone else, the *teachers of music* have to experience the consequences of a want of skill and strength in the hands of many learners, and they know how greatly a systematic educational training of the fingers and hands for the

very best means of overcoming the technical difficulties."—Schmidt's *"Annals of Medicine."*

"Technical difficulties will most safely and quickly be conquered by proper gymnastic exercises of the hand and fingers."—Dr. Dietz, *"Member of the Royal Council of Medicine."*

"To obtain technical skill and muscular steadiness, a gymnastic education is the best means."—P. M. Link.

"The gymnast exercises his limbs through preparatory exercises; how, therefore, is it possible for the player of the piano and violin to dispense with this gymnastic preparation of the joints of the hand and fingers?"—Prof. Rector v. Schmidt, *"President of the Royal Gymnasium."*

"La souplesse et l'étendue des poignets dépendent du développement gymnastique des forces. La gymnastique développe l'aisance et la grâce."—Dr. M. Bally.

"For so great an art as piano or violin playing, the muscles of the fingers are weak; they ought to be *prepared* by proper gymnastic exercises."—Ferguson.

execution of the more delicate movements is needed.

Nevertheless, there are many arts besides music for which the hand ought to be also trained from early youth, in order to be able permanently to accomplish, in later years, what is excellent, *e. g.*, many kinds of handicraft, machine-work, needle-work, anatomy and surgery, writing and drawing, and all fine manipulations.

An untrained hand will either remain clumsy in these branches of work, or it will soon fail through over-exertion, which causes a peculiar kind of paralysis, connected with cramp, and well known to writers (the so-called writers' cramp), but which also affects musicians, artists, shoemakers, tailors, sempstresses, and other working people. Certain it is, that if this matter had been inquired into before, and public attention directed to it, a great deal of trouble and vexation in learning music might have been saved; the labour of many working people of all classes, who chiefly have to use their fingers, have been greatly facilitated; and, moreover, many diseases of the joints of the fingers and hand might have been prevented.

CHAPTER V.

To become a skillful musician is no small matter.
There is no art which demands more labour,
patience, and especially more *time*, than, for
instance, piano or violin playing; and at least
half of that time is for years required for the
particular purpose of strengthening the muscles
of the fingers, and rendering them flexible.
And why so many years? Because the muscles,
the ligaments, and the tendons of the finger-
joints and wrists have not previously been gymnastically exercised and trained.

To prove in a practical manner that it is
particularly important to prepare the muscles
and ligaments of the fingers and hand, I will
cite a fact which may appear startling, but
which, nevertheless, is true, viz., that the
muscles and tendons of the fingers, in spite
of their great importance, are, proportionately
speaking, the least of all practised in daily
life.

Take all sorts of people from amongst the
labouring classes, such as the smith, the joiner,

the gardener, the bricklayer, the stone-mason, the husbandman, the day-labourer, etc., etc. They are at work the whole day, and acquire arms like steel and muscle like giants; but they very *rarely* use the *fingers*, which, there-fore, remain unexercised. And it is the same with the educated classes, without difference of age or sex.

This is the reason why the learning of piano and violin playing is attended with such great difficulties, and why the muscles and ligaments of the hand ought to be trained by proper gymnastic exercises. For their weakness arises, for physiological reasons, from the very fact of their inactivity

This fact I will satisfactorily prove in the sequel, for it forms the basis and key of my discoveries.

CHAPTER VI.

THE PRINCIPAL DIFFICULTY DOES NOT CONSIST IN THE
READING OF MUSIC, BUT IN THE WEAKNESS OF THE
FINGERS.

IN the opinion of many, the chief difficulty to
be overcome in studying music consists in learning
to *read* it. But this is by no means the case. The
reading of music is learned in the same manner as
a child learns to read letters. The first difficulties
having been mastered, the task is easy; as with
a printed book, so with music.

Consequently the paramount difficulty is not in
the *notes*, but in the weakness and *awkwardness of
the fingers* and wrists. From this, again, it may be
plainly seen how necessary it is to train the *fingers*
before commencing the work of the *head*. In
short, what is wanted is a regular gymnastic
training for the muscles of the fingers, the joints,
and the wrists; and it will be found that the
following exercises, being as desirable as they are
applicable for every age, will strengthen and
render them flexible in a most surprising manner;
will materially shorten the time of study, and save
much labour; nevertheless, on that account, *the
ordinary finger-practice, scales and studies, should
of course* NOT *be omitted.*

Suppose a boy from 10 to 14 years old, who is strong and healthy by means of gymnastics and other exercises, set to learn the piano or violin. His body is strong with gymnastic exercises, but his wrists and *fingers* are weak and awkward. How is he, with the method now in use, to succeed in playing an instrument well, without very long and wearying work? No wonder that the painful exertion almost makes him despair, and that finally he gives up the thing altogether. But if, on the contrary, his fingers and joints have been gymnastically trained and exercised beforehand, he will get on easily and quickly, and continue his studies with pleasure.

Many presidents and teachers of the most celebrated gymnastic institutions have, therefore, come to the determination to introduce into their establishments these exercises, in addition to the other branches of gymnastic training. Their practical utility for all those who work with their fingers, for anatomists, surgeons, sculptors, watchmakers, and many others, is as evident as their salutary effect, from a medical point of view, in curvature and paralysis of the hand and forearm, in weakness of the muscles and nerves, writers' cramp, and similar complaints, is undeniable.

CHAPTER VII.

MUSIC IS THE ART WHICH MAKES THE HIGHEST DEMANDS
ON THE MUSCLES OF THE FINGERS. — MOVING THE FINGERS
UP AND DOWN INSUFFICIENT.

THESE exercises for persons engaged in musical
pursuits can, least of all, be dispensed with, because music is the art which makes the highest
demands on the muscles of the fingers and wrists.

Eminent physiologists say, "Gymnastic exercises
for the fingers and joints ought to have been commenced 150 years ago; they form the real foundation of practical art."

It is, indeed, incredible that so great an art as
piano and violin playing should have arrived at
so high a stage of perfection without a previous
training of the muscles.

CHAPTER VIII.

ARTISTS AND TEACHERS OF MUSIC.

IF any one should say that he has diligently studied the piano and violin after the method used at present, and in course of time has learned and taught it with the greatest success without having found it necessary to trouble himself about any other system; my reply is, that music is one of the most beautiful, and with respect to muscular work, the most difficult of arts, and that all the arts and sciences, music not excepted, have made enormous strides in advance during the present century. But exactly because music has become a universal boon for all classes of the civilized world, one ought to be so much the *less* disposed to *shut out* new ideas respecting it, from whatever side they may come. The most highly honoured are those who have made the greatest progress in theory and in practice, or who have readily and generously acknowledged such progress from all sides.

It is, therefore, the duty of all to assist teachers of music and proficients, as much as possible, in promoting this beautiful accomplishment; for this reason, encouraged by persons of the highest distinction, and moved by the love of the art and

of mankind, I humbly venture to make known my
"Gymnastics of the Fingers and Wrist," and to
offer to all who work with their fingers in general,
and to musicians in particular, a means which,
based on physiological principles, leals most
surely to the attainment of artistic execution, and
which is in itself so simple that any child may use
it; a means, too, which will effect a great saving
of time, and facilitate the work of both teachers
and students.

I have only to add that, as a matter of course,
these exercises, in order to have the desired effect,
must be carried out *gymnastically and regularly,*
according to *the directions* given, and not otherwise : whilst on the other hand, they ought not
to be carried to excess, *nor are they intended to
supersede the usual finger exercises, scales, and
studies.*

CHAPTER IX.

First Movement.

STRETCH the fingers as much as possible one from
the other, let them fall on the large muscle of the

Fig. 5.   Fig. 6.

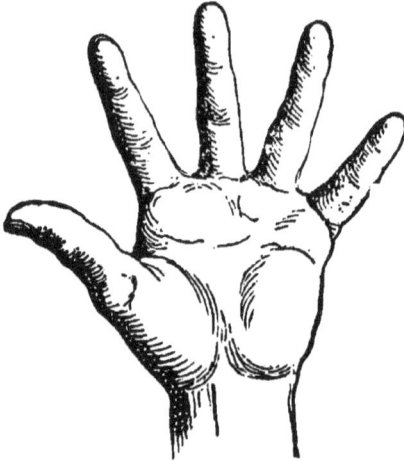 

thumb (thumb-ball), and press them firmly on it;
remain for a moment in this position, and bring
the thumb against the forefinger, 40 times up and
down.

You will find that this exercise, as well as

several others, if vigorously continued for three minutes only, is very fatiguing; a clear proof that the muscles of the fingers, although they may be quite fit for ordinary daily occupations, are, nevertheless, *very weak and incapable* when anything more is demanded from them, and without proper gymnastic training, they must remain so.

SECOND MOVEMENT

Fig. 7.   Fig. 8.

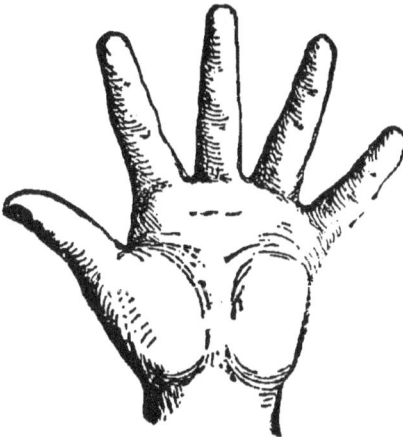 

Stretch the fingers as before, but let the finger-ends fall against the middle of the cavity of the hand, instead of against the great muscle of the thumb, and press them firmly. To be repeated 40 times.

THIRD MOVEMENT.

The following exercise (Figs. 9 and 10), is intended particularly for the small joints of the fingers. It is effective, but difficult.

c 2

Fig. 9.   Fig. 10.

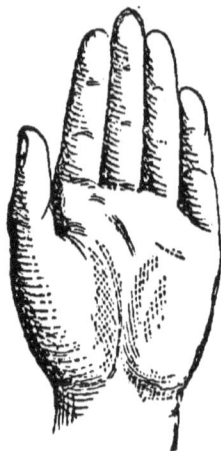 

Do not stretch the fingers away from one another, but hold them firmly, and close together.
as this produces the effect particularly desired.
Bend the two first finger-joints of the four fingers
closely together; move them vigorously up and
down, and press them on *firmly*, without, however, moving the large joints. Repeat this movement until you are tired, which will not be long,
thus affording another practical proof how weak
the untrained finger-joints are. This is also an
excellent exercise for the thumb, provided it is
made slowly and vigorously. It may also be made
with outstretched fingers.

I again repeat that no one who has not already
tried the above or similar exercises of the fingers,
will be able vigorously to continue them for even
so short a time as three minutes without experien-
cing painful fatigue. And why? Because, as I have

demonstrated before, the joints of the fingers and
wrists are, in the ordinary occupations of life, the
least of all exercised, and consequently the weakest in comparison with what they have afterwards
to perform.

After this experience, people will, in future, hardly
venture to teach and to continue the exercise of an
art like music (which, from a muscular point of view,
is the most difficult of all), with muscles the weakest
and least trained, without having previously prepared them by proper gymnastic exercises.

FOURTH MOVEMENT.

The last free exercise for the finger-joints,
which I will recommend here (Figs. 11 and 12),

Fig. 11.

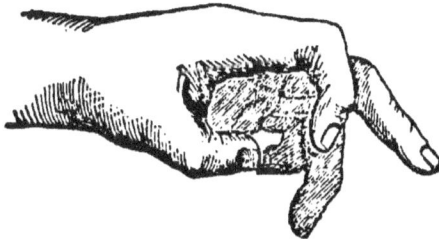

Fig. 12.

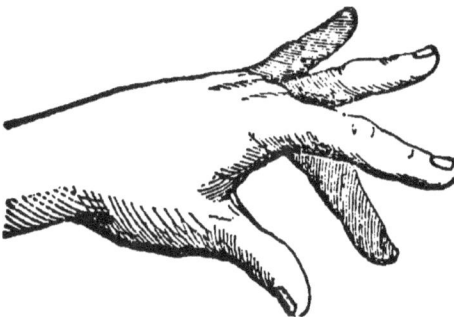

consists in moving all the fingers and the thumb, one after the other, stretching them far away from one another, like claws, and alternately bending and raising them in whatever direction you please, and as long as you like or are able, but always vigorously.

CHAPTER X.

ALTHOUGH it is not easy to prescribe complete gymnastic exercises for the thumb, the following, if made vigorously, will, nevertheless, be found very effective.

FIRST MOVEMENT.

Fig. 13.   Fig. 14.

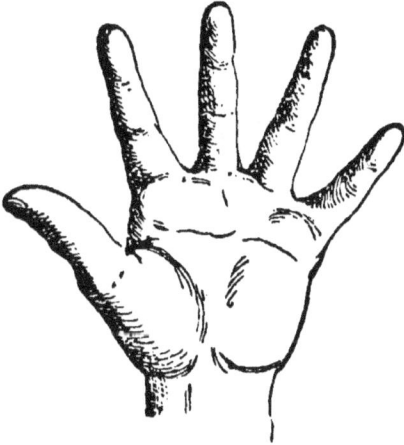 

Stretch the fingers as far as possible away from one another, then press the hand firmly together, the thumb being held fast in the cavity of the hand; continue for a moment in this position, and then repeat the same movement, alternately opening and closing the hand.

SECOND MOVEMENT.

Fig. 15.

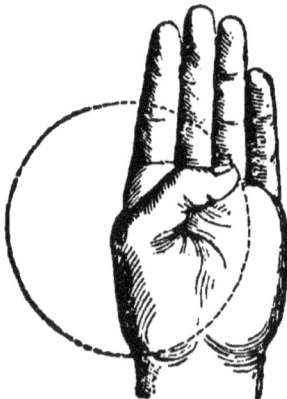

Hold the fingers close together, stretch out the thumb, and then perform with the latter a circular movement inside the hand, first 20 times to the right, then 20 times to the left: to be repeated again and again.

THIRD MOVEMENT.

Fig. 16

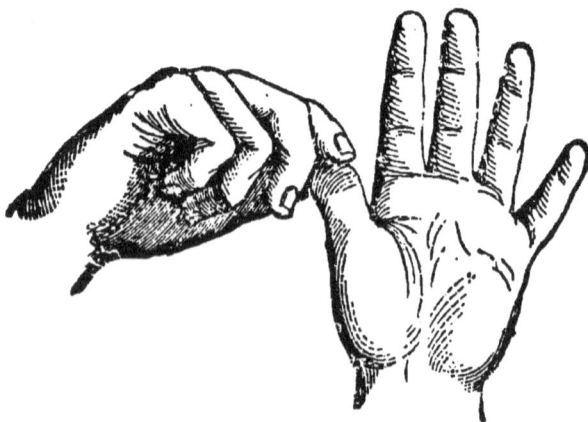

Take hold of the thumb of the one hand with the fingers of the other, or with the whole hand, and shake it or bend it to its root, without, however, overdoing either.

In short, perform every day some exercise with the thumb and fingers, whereby they will be sufficiently brought into exercise.

CHAPTER XI.

FIRST MOVEMENT.

Fig. 17.   Fig. 18.

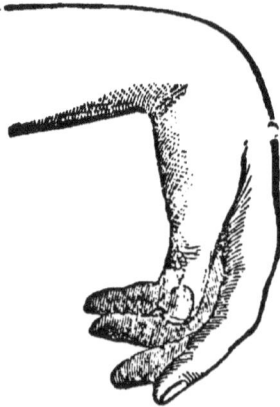 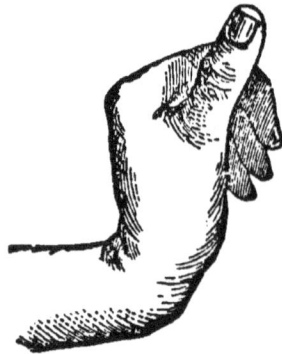

MOVE the wrist, *without moving the arm or elbow*, vigorously up and down in a perpendicular direction, from 20 to 40 times, first slowly, then more quickly; finally, as quick as possible. In doing so, let the elbows rest close to the body, so as to bring both hands and wrists into the proper position. As soon as you are tired, leave off.

SECOND MOVEMENT.

Fig. 19.　　　　　　Fig. 20.

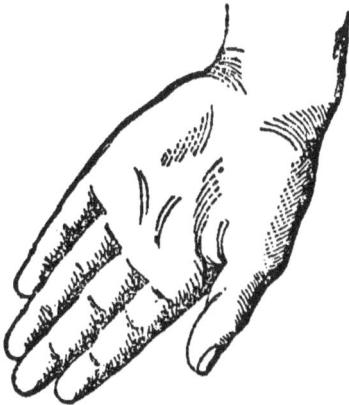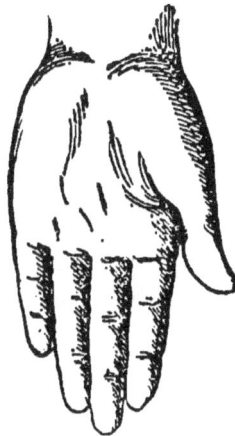

Move the hand horizontally or vertically without moving the arm.

To understand the practical utility of this exercise (Figs. 19, 20), it ought to be borne in mind that the entire action of the wrist is effected by two principal joints, one of which, the smaller of the two, lies at the root of the hand, and is called the "joint of the hand," by means of which it becomes possible to move the hand, independently of the arm, at its root. The other joint, the larger of the two, rises from the elbow, and is called the rotatory joirt of the forearm. Holding, then, all the five fingers close together, move the smaller joint perpendicularly or horizontally, as you please, without in any way moving the arm, and at the same time holding the elbow close to the body.

THIRD MOVEMENT.

Fig. 21.   Fig. 22.

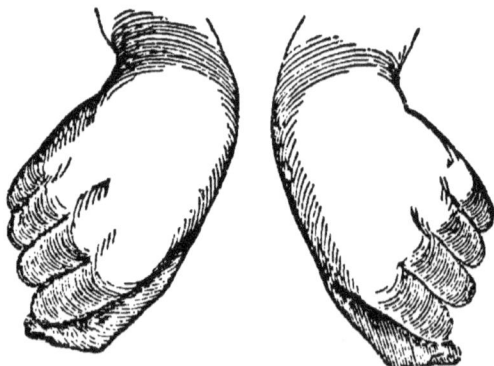

Move the wrists in a slanting direction right and left, as above, first slowly, then quicker and quicker. Hold the elbows as before. By this movement both the joints mentioned above will be put into action (Figs. 21, 22).

The young violinist, who generally finds the sideways movement of the wrist of the right hand so difficult, will derive great advantage from all these wrist exercises.

Holding your arm quite still, move the free hand or fist vigorously round in a circle, 20 times to the right, and 20 times to the left, first slowly, then more quickly. By this exercise all the muscles of the hand and the arm will be put into motion; and though the most difficult of all, this is at the same time one of the most important exercises.

All these several free movements of the hand and fingers may be repeated *many times* with advantage; still, by simply performing them, short though they be, daily and regularly, the prescribed time

only, the desired end of strengthening the muscles
of the fingers and wrists, and rendering them
vigorous and flexible, will be surely attained.

FOURTH MOVEMENT.

Fig. 23.

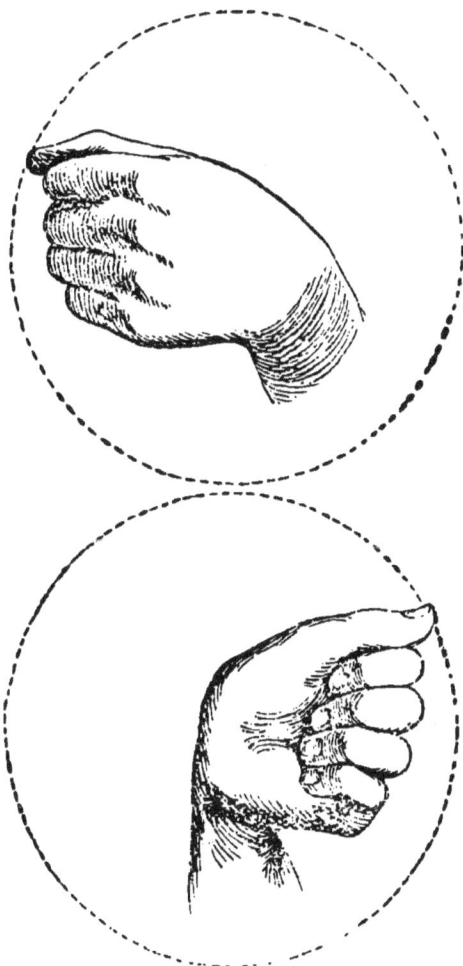

I could mention some other free exercises of
the fingers; but those already described will be
sufficient for general use.

CHAPTER XII

FIRST MOVEMENT.

Fig. 24.   Fig. 25.

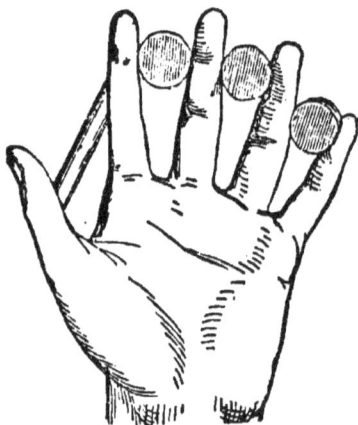 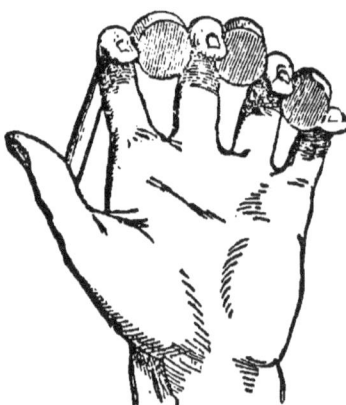

TAKE for each hand three cork cylinders, three quarters of an inch long, and from half to one inch in diameter, according to the size of the fingers; place them between the upper ends of the fingers, and while gradually and conveniently extending the muscles, by bending the fingers, move the latter as shown by the above figures, 24 and 25.

Move the cylinders further down, to the roots of the fingers, and perform the exercises according to Figs. 26 and 27. In doing this, put a small round

SECOND MOVEMENT.

Fig. 26.

Fig. 27.

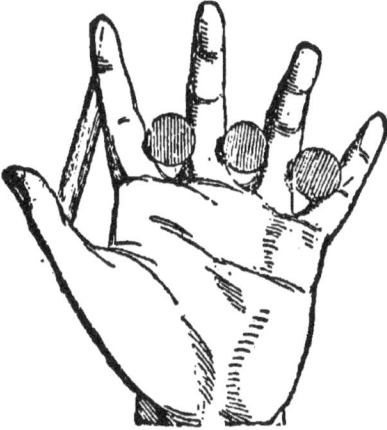
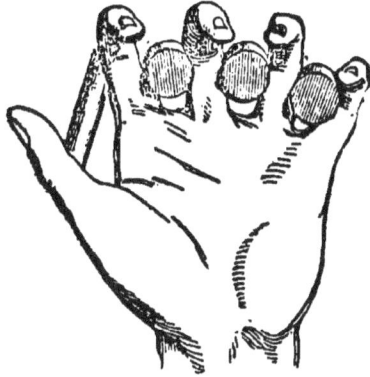

piece of wood between the thumb and the fore-
finger, at a distance sufficient to extend the former
as much as possible.

Leaving the other fingers as before, put a large
cylinder between the thumb and fore-finger (Figs. 28

THIRD MOVEMENT.

Fig. 28.

Fig. 29.

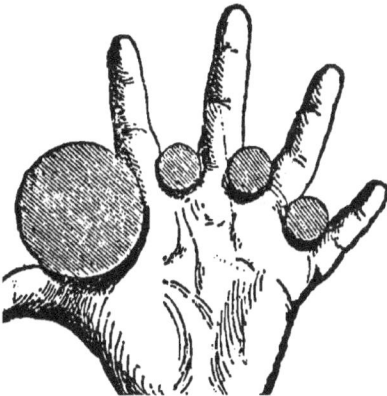
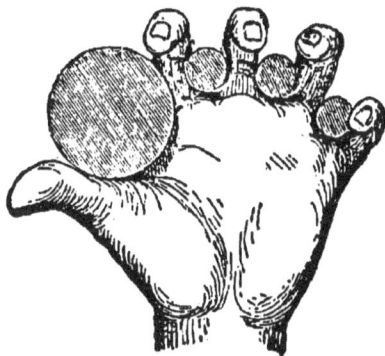

and 29), so as to entirely fill up the intervening space. In doing this, be careful to extend the thumb as much as possible. In case the tension of the fingers is small, take smaller cylinders; or if the latter should be too hard for tender hands, cover them with some soft substance, such as velvet, or the like.

Perform all these exercises vigorously, and, if possible, just before practising the musical instrument, twice or three times daily, each time for a few minutes, especially in the morning, on getting up. As a matter of course, after eight or ten hours' rest, the muscles of the fingers and wrist, like those of the rest of the body, are somewhat stiff, and ought to be prepared by proper gymnastic exercises, before beginning to play. Besides, *provided over-exertion be avoided*, there is not, according to the best medical authorities, the least danger to be apprehended from these exercises, for the joints and muscles of even the very smallest hands.

If players of the piano and violin should object that, in the act of *playing*, the fingers need not be so much extended as prescribed here, or assert that the finger-exercises, scales, and *études* as at present used are perfectly sufficient, and that nothing more is wanted, I can only repeat, that the fingers must be *prepared* in order to render them strong and flexible; that, for this purpose, it is necessary to exercise them *gymnastically*, and that, as I have explained before, these preparatory exercises will save much time and trouble, and facilitate the work of both teachers and pupils; *further*—that, by the diligent practice of these gymnastics, the fingers become elastic and independent of each other; you acquire thereby complete control over them, and *when you have* done *this*, you can move them and do with them as *you* will.

ANOTHER MOST EFFECTIVE mode of stretching and loosening the tendons and ligaments which encompass the large middle-hand bones, or "knuckles," may be performed as follows:—

Place the forefinger of each hand, up to the middle joint, firmly on the table and in that position press it up and down with a certain degree of force, for a few seconds; then withdraw it, and apply the next finger in a precisely similar manner; then the two other fingers in succession, each finger remaining on the table alone, unaccompanied by any other.

Afterwards, apply the 2nd and 4th together, exactly in the same way, for a few seconds; then the 3rd and 5th; lastly the thumb.

The pupil may do this many times a day with great advantage; for by this process the ligaments and tendons of the knuckles are stretched and loosened, and the muscles are set free.

Of course always with due moderation.

ANOTHER VERY IMPORTANT exercise, bearing chiefly

on the tendons and ligaments of the large metacarpal joints or knuckles, is the following:—

With the thumb and fore-finger of the one hand
take hold of one finger of the other hand, and
shake it up and down, for one minute, to its root.
Then take the other fingers in succession in like
manner. To be applied equally to both hands, and
to be done, especially with the 4th and 5th fingers,
separately, as often as leisure permits.

To this category belongs also ANOTHER EXERCISE
of the metacarpal joints or knuckles. Into the
palm of one outstretched hand place the closed
fingers or fist of the other; then open and close
the *latter* as fast and as long a time as is agreeable, always continuing to press upon the palm.
Change hands and repeat. Ever remember that
the difficulties of bringing the fingers into order
lie, physiologically, almost all in the *middle-hand
bones* or knuckles; and as the five preceding exercises—and especially the three last—act in a very
efficient and special manner upon the ligaments,
tendons, and muscles of these joints, they *cannot
be made too often.*

CHAPTER XIII.

MECHANICAL FINGER-EXERCISES (CONTINUED).

IT is not sufficient to play the ordinary finger-exercises and scales. As has been shown in the opening chapters, and in the anatomical representations of the hand, all the fingers are not equally strong; for instance, the 4th and 5th fingers are, by nature, much weaker than the others, and it is necessary to remedy this inequality.

Each finger ought, therefore, to have gymnastic exercises *for itself*, and they ought to be performed on some solid body, which can be firmly grasped. For this purpose take a round staff, from 12 to 18 inches long, and half to three quarters of an inch thick, on which, at a proper distance from one another, round indentations are made, and into which the fingers are to be placed after the manner illustrated in the following figures.

D 2

Fig. 30.

DIRECTIONS.

Place the thumb of each hand on one side, and the four fingers *very firmly* fixed on the other side of the staff; *raise one finger as high as possible*, and let it fall down vigorously, like a hammer, twenty times in succession, while the three remaining fingers, *stretched out from one another*, like claws, remain immovable. In the same way exercise the other fingers; firmly, *slowly*, vigorously, and immediately after the cylinder exercises just described. Repeat this three times daily, each time for five minutes, altogether for fifteen minutes a day, *but the oftener it be done the better*.

Those playing the piano need not confine themselves to one particular exercise, but may make use of all the figures at pleasure.

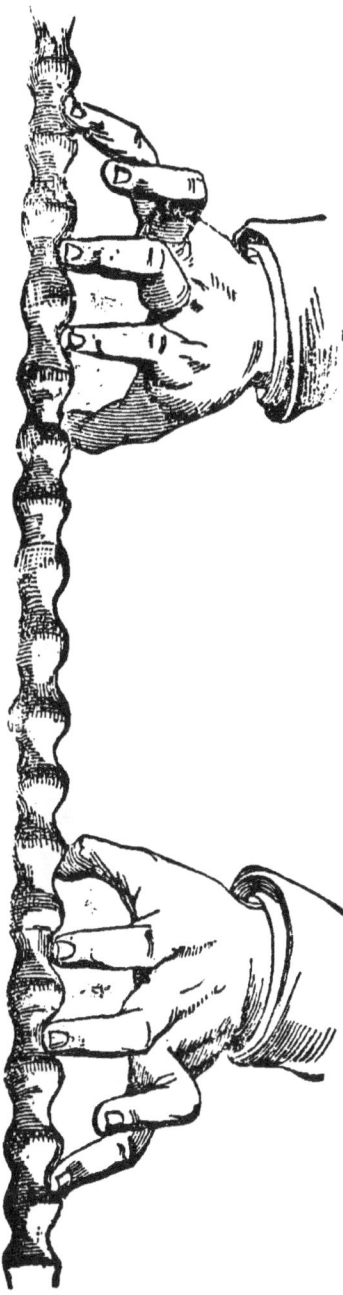

Fig. 31.

Fig. 32.

Fig. 33.

Fig. 34.

The fingers of the left hand may also be trained
for violin playing, as seen in Fig. 35.

Fig. 35.

FURTHER UPON THE SAME. — After the cylinders,
by far the most effective of all means for imparting, gymnastically, strength and flexibility to the
fingers, together with evenness of vigour, individuality. and independence, is, daily, in the room,
or while walking, to take the above-named staff,
or, indeed, a smooth round stick of 18 inches
long, and half to three quarters of an inch thick,
or an ordinary walking-stick, and to perform on it
as follows: — With the four fingers of one or both
hands firmly pressed and stretched upon it, raise
one finger as high as possible, and, as above stated,
let it fall down upon it vigorously, like a hammer,

while the other fingers remain firmly pressed on
the stick, twenty to thirty times in succession, then
in couplets with the 5th and 4th fingers, then with
the 4th and 3rd, then with the 3rd and 2nd, twenty
times each, the two fingers, in all cases, as stated,
lifted as high as possible, and the others remaining,
stretched at even distances, firm upon the staff,
finally, with the four fingers of each hand, twelve
times ascending and 12 times descending, but
always SLOWLY, energetically, with firm pressure,
"and in time." You may *occasionally* practise a
little faster, but it must be the exception. Slow
moving, pressing, and stretching should form the
chief gymnastic rule.*   This staff may be *perfectly
plain*, or *indented*.

In a similar manner you may practise, *slowly
and with energy*, with one or with both hands,
all sorts of difficult muscular movements and passages upon the staff, for example: —

FIRST SERIES. In couplets twenty to thirty *times
each in succession*, with the 2nd and 4th fingers,
alternating, afterwards, with the 4th and 2nd; then
with the 3rd and 5th fingers, alternating with the 5th
and 3rd; in each case the two fingers stretched wide
apart, and the other fingers pressed upon the staff.

SECOND SERIES.   In couplets twenty to thirty

* The late Mr. Clementi was celebrated for the perfect evenness
and beauty of his touch in playing rapid passages on the piano. The
means by which he attained this execution he was unwilling to
disclose. It is now known that he effected it by playing his scales
VERY SLOWLY, and with *great pressure* of each individual finger
(see page 70).

times each in succession, with the 2nd and 3rd
fingers, first close together, then wide apart, afterwards alternating, in the same way, with the 3rd
and 2nd. With the 3rd and 4th fingers, first close
together, then wide apart, afterwards alternating,
in the same way, with the 4th and 3rd. With
the 4th and 5th fingers, first close together, then
wide apart, afterwards alternating in the same
way with the 5th and 4th. In each case slowly,
the two fingers lifted as high as is convenient,
twenty to thirty times in succession, and the other
fingers firmly fixed upon the staff. Lastly, all
the four fingers together, in each of these varied
and different directions.

The number of times of each movement, and
the duration of time, also whether all should be
made at the same hour, or otherwise, is left to
the discretion of the teacher and pupil. I would
recommend, at first, the selection of three or four
modes or exercises, for persistent practice, to last
over a given period of time, then to change to others.

But the regular exercise of the whole or part
of them, *daily*, will, in a comparatively short time,
most surely impart immense strength to, and render
flexible, the muscles and joints of the fingers; will
enable you, if the directions be duly followed, to
effect for yourself perfectly equal and even fingering,
and render the fingers entirely *independent one of
another*.

But let all be done with due moderation, and
not driven to excess.

This gymnastic staff, or walking-stick exercise. however simple it may appear, should, on no account, any single day be omitted. It produces a most surprising effect if carefully and vigorously made; an effect which will be the more remarkable in proportion as the fingers are pressed and stretched far away from one another. By this means all the various muscles, and even the tendons, joints, and ligaments are put in motion, and both fingers and nerves are rendered strong and firm. Besides, no time need be lost; as in performing these exercises you may converse or engage in other occupations.

In this manner, also, *the 4th finger may* have a special training, and become equally strong with the others. This finger is, on physiological grounds, the weakest of all, and after a number of vain attempts at remedying its well-known weakness, some physiologists in Germany have gone so far as to suggest the idea whether it would not be well to cut the ligament joining the two fingers, in order to set the 4th finger free.

But it is unnecessary to have recourse to such rude and unnatural measures; the natural weakness of the 4th finger may be effectually remedied, and may be entirely overcome, by the above exercises.

These exercises may be *partially* performed on musical instruments; but they are *far more* effective if made as directed; because the fingers, in having a resting point, or lever, and having something firm to grasp, are enabled to perform them *gymnastically*

CHAPTER XIV.

MOREOVER, beautiful works of art, like pianofortes, violins, and other musical instruments, ought not to be used as gymnastic implements. The fingers and joints ought, therefore *first*, to be gymnastically exercised; *then* play upon the instrument.

The head and the fingers ought to go together; but how is this possible if the latter remain behind? The mind strives forward, the fingers keep it back. Why should this torture be inflicted? No; let the fingers first be properly trained, then head and fingers will go harmoniously together.

Another great advantage attending the above exercises is, that the organs of hearing are spared. Many persons, who zealously and perseveringly perform finger-exercises on musical instruments, injure their health, through the irritation of the auditory nerves, to such a degree as either to be prevented, on medical authority, from continuing to practise, or otherwise to be subjected to serious consequences; whereas, if the exercises are preceded by the *gymnastic* movements given above, the hearing organs of the pupil will be greatly spared, and not injured in any way.

The greatest technical art consists in controlling alike the fingers, the joints, and the nerves. Now, if the muscles and tendons are exercised and strengthened by proper physical work, the *nerves* will be invigorated at the same time. This is a well-known fact, and for those engaged in musical pursuits, **an** advantage which it is impossible **to** overrate. The fingers will not then be fatigued **as** easily as before, and you learn at the same time by habit to acquire complete control over them.

Nor ought another advantage to be overlooked; viz., that in regard to artists and persons who play well, when these travel, or from any other cause are *prevented* from playing for some time on a musical instrument, they will be enabled, in the manner described above, to exercise efficiently for a short time daily their fingers and joints. Thus they will not get stiff, and you will always remain their master.

However, to attain this end, the exercises **on** the stick ought not to be performed carelessly, but *gymnastically*, and STRICTLY *according to the directions given above.*

The same exercises are very useful for persons playing the violin, by promoting the proper bending of the *fore-finger* of the left hand.

Generally speaking, the whole of the above exercises are equally fit for all persons playing the piano, the organ, the violin, the violoncello, and other instruments; and they will find, after having accustomed themselves to perform them vigorously

for a short time daily, that they then come tc
the instrument with a strength and individuality
of finger which will exceed their utmost ex-
pectations.

CHAPTER XV.

TAKE a board, about 22 inches long, 4 to 5 inches wide, and three-quarters of an inch thick, and mark out on it four or five grooves, about half an inch deep. To fix this board on a table, have a little ledge glued on to one of its sides, as in Figs. 36 and 37.

Place the outstretched hand on the board; stretch the thumb and the little finger as far as possible away from one another, into one of the grooves, place the other fingers into one of the other grooves, and set them in motion, while holding the thumb and little finger firmly in their places.

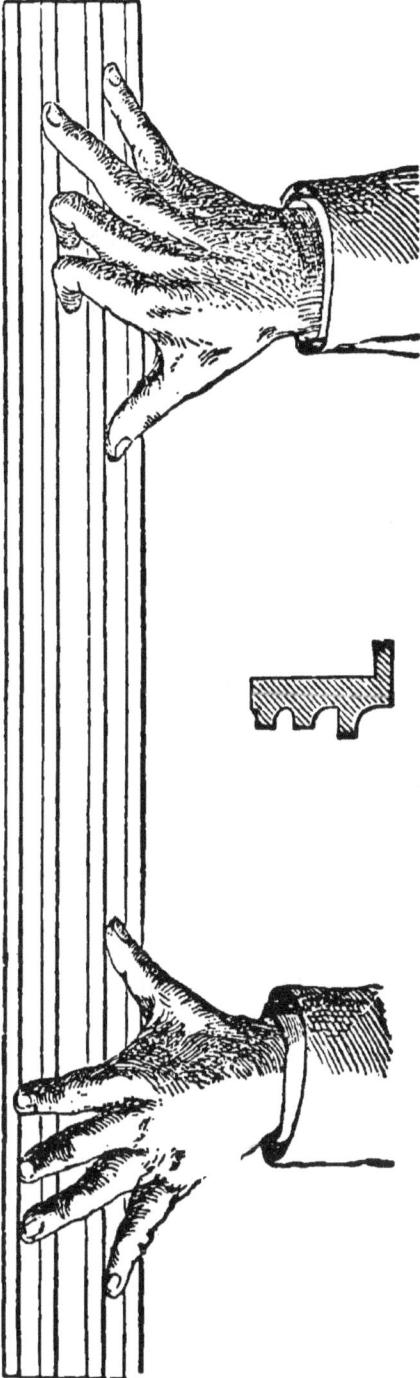

Fig. 26.

Fig. 27.

CHAPTER XVI.

The following mechanical gymnastic exercises
refer to the *wrist of the right hand*, and are intended for players on stringed instruments. Their chief
purpose is to render the wrist of the right hand
and fore-arm strong and flexible. This all students
find very difficult; it will soon be evident for
what reason.

It is a fact acknowledged by the most celebrated
musicians, that the principal bowing difficulties in
playing the violin arise from the wrist. This is
chiefly owing to the circumstance that, in playing
the violin, the movement *sideways* of the wrist is a
peculiar one, being, in fact, totally different from
any other movements taking place in the ordinary
occupations of life. If, therefore, it be desired to
diminish the painful work, as customary at present,
it is indispensable to *prepare* the wrist and arm by
exercises like those we are about to describe.

Take, three times daily, and particularly early in
the morning, a *light stick or cane*, exceeding the
length of a violin bow by 8—10 inches, holding it
in your right hand the same as a bow; lay it on
the left hand — which is to be raised to the same

height as if playing the violin or violoncello – and move it *vigorously* up and down as follows:—

1. The entire length, thirty times.

2. The middle length; with the fore-arm and wrist only, without moving the upper arm, thirty— forty times.

3. At the *nutt*; with the wrist alone— and especially up-stroke—with energy; without in the least moving the arm, thirty—forty times.

4. At the extreme *head*-end; with the wrist alone, and with pressure; without in the least moving the arm, thirty—forty times.

Move the cane alternately up and down, pressing it with the thumb and fore-finger, and look at the direction of the wrist and the stick or cane. With this cane you may exercise gymnastically, at pleasure, up and down strokes, triplets, and all sorts of bow-movements. The effect you will find surprising.

These exercises are particularly useful for the student. As a matter of course, they can also be *partially* made with the bow, but *not with the same effect.*

CHAPTER XVII.

THERE is another very effective gymnastic exercise for strengthening and rendering flexible the wrist of the right hand. A movement resembling it has already been described above, but to prevent any misconception, I think it well to give explicit directions respecting it here.

Take hold (with your *right* hand) of the end of a *long and rather heavy Alpenstock*, and work it vigorously up and down, *like a bow*, upon the *left* hand (upheld near the chin) in the following manner:

1. With the *whole arm*, from the elbow, up and down, with the stick, thirty times.

2. With the *middle length* of the stick, up and down, twenty-five times.

3. With the stick as near as *possible* at the *lower* end, with the *wrist alone*, and *without* in any way *moving the arm*, thirty times.

4. Ditto at the *upper* end, with the *wrist alone*, especially for the *up-stroke*, without in any way moving the arm, thirty times.

This exercise, on anatomical grounds, produces a considerable effect on the muscles and sinews of the wrist and the fore-arm, in imparting to them the wished-for strength and flexibility.

Besides, it is a well-known fact that, having handled a heavy object, it is more easy skilfully to handle a lighter one.

If it should be objected that the last-mentioned gymnastic exercises, being of rather a rough kind, might spoil the elegant stroke, my answer is, that those so-called rough exercises only last a very short time daily, and are undertaken for the *special* purpose of rendering the arm and wrist strong, easy, even, and flexible. Indeed, if these right-hand exercises are made *carefully* and *according to the directions given*, a short time every day, they will strengthen the wrist of the right hand, and render it pliant and flexible to such a degree, as to enable persons, in a comparatively short time, to play with the wrist almost as vigorously as with the arm.

There is, moreover, another advantage attending these exercises, viz., that, if continued for *some weeks only*, and for a *few minutes daily*, they will soon give the proper position to the student's arm, which, consequently, will not be required to be tied to the body, as was often done in former times

CHAPTER XVIII.

CONTINUATION.—STACCATO.

A famous German chamber violinist once remarked to me, "I find that staccato playing is the best exercise for bowing, but I can't say why." The reason, however, lies in the fact that, by frequently playing with the end of the bow, or with the staccato-stroke, the muscles of the wrist are put in motion, thus undergoing a *gymnastic* training by which strength and flexibility are acquired.

It is *impossible* to perform the staccato-stroke well unless the muscles of the wrist have become *strong and agile*; and the reason why the student finds this stroke in most cases so difficult is, that the wrist has *not* been specially trained and prepared, in consequence of which it remains weak and stiff.

It ought to be remembered that in almost all kinds of handiwork in daily life, the *whole* arm is active and in motion, and *very rarely* the *wrist alone*. With musical instruments, on the contrary, and particularly in playing the violin, it is necessary *always* to use the wrist, and it is *impossible* to play well unless the wrist has been rendered strong and elastic. It is, therefore, absolutely indispensable that proper gymnastic exercises should be made with the wrist, in order to *prepare it*. The wrist, indeed, ought to be *accustomed*, in other words, *to move of itself*, and the student ought, as often as possible, to perform all kinds of movements calcu- lated to impart to it pliancy and strength. It will then soon become free and easy, and the student will, in the course of time, acquire the strongest, most elegant, and artistic stroke.

No single one of these practical gymnastic exercises ought to be despised on account of its simplicity. *Only* try them, and they will be found very effective. All sensible artists and teachers will do homage to every improvement, and con- sider it their duty to welcome any assistance calculated to diminish and render lighter the arduous toil, and shorten the valuable time re- quired for becoming a proficient in music.

CHAPTER XIX.

CONCLUDING REMARKS.

I will only add, in conclusion, that it would be well not to continue too long with the same gymnastic exercise, but to allow the muscles and joints some change, which will be found both agreeable and advantageous. If, therefore, the student be tired of one exercise, he should begin another. Besides, if the fingers are fatigued and hot by playing, and the nerves irritated, an exercise of some of the different free or mechanical gymnastic appliances will refresh the muscles, by imparting to them a new and an easier movement. And be it remembered, "these exercises are not irksome, but recreative."

To sum up: No student ought to begin to learn or to play the piano, violin, or other musical instrument, or even to engage in any work or occupation requiring a strong and flexible hand, before having set the joints of his fingers and hands in order, by means of preparatory gymnastic exercises; and he ought to continue the same from day to day.

Let it ever be borne in mind that much rapid playing affects injuriously the muscles and nerves;

while, on the other hand *slow exercises and studies* invigorate them.

To borrow an illustration from the animal world; take the race-horse, the fleetest animal which we use in this country, whose great task requires that his muscles should be brought into the highest condition of strength and flexibility. Do **you** suppose that, in training and preparing him for the race—a process often extending over a considerable period—that he is, in the course of it, much galloped? By no means! Galloping forms the exception, and, during this long interval, walking, trotting, and cantering, form his chief training paces; namely, four-fifths or seven-eighths of the time! galloping only one-fifth or one eighth part! His skilful trainer knows that much rapid exertion, such as galloping *long continued*, weakens and wears out his muscle. So, also, in the hunting-field and on the road, it is "the pace that kills." Even so with the player upon a musical instrument; long continued, rapid movements, wear out the muscle and shake the nerves, while slow exercises, however vigorously executed, invigorate and strengthen both. (*See p. 66, note on* CLEMENTI.)

And here I avail myself of this opportunity to raise a question for consideration regarding that part of the violin bow which the right thumb presses. Let me ask, *first,* why should this little sharp projection be permitted to appear on every bow, to the prejudice of the placing firmly the thumb there, instead of being *rounded off?* and, *secondly,* why should there not be placed, close to this point, especially for students, a small piece of round gutta percha—a gutta percha button—as a *stay* to the thumb? Great facility would thus be afforded for holding the bow firmly. Any one may put a piece of gutta percha in the candle. and, when softened, stick it fast on the place indic ted.

Finally, I repeat that, in performing any of these gymnastic exercises, the principal condition to be adhered to is, that they should always be made in the morning, also immediately before playing; and that while great vigour is imparted by fodowing out strictly the directions given, any over-exertion should be avoided. As to the claims of the author himself, they are limited to an earnest desire that his "Gymnastics of the Fingers and Wrist," founded as they are on anatomical and physiological principles, may find favour with the public, and be instrumental in promoting the best interests of art.

E. WARD-JACKSON, J.P.

TESTIMONIALS.

From PRESCOTT HEWETT, F.R C.S., *Surgeon to St. George's Hospital, late Professor of Anatomy to R.C.S.*

Aug. 28th, 1865.

"Having carefully examined the gymnastic exercises invented by Mr. Edwin Ward-Jackson for the due working of the fingers and hand, I have great pleasure in stating that I believe that such exercises will be of the greatest use, not only to musicians, but to every one who wishes to possess a perfectly free use of his hands. The power and the freedom obtainable by exercises such as these have been little thought of; but from what I have seen, I feel confident that Mr. Jackson's exercises, if rightly used, are destined to make the hand much more perfect for all its purposes than it really is."

From LUTHER HOLDEN. F.R.C.S., *Senior Lecturer on Anatomy at St. Bartholomew's Hospital.*

Aug. 28th, 1865.

"Since our last interview I have often thought and talked about the practical effect of your 'Gymnastic Exercises for the Fingers.' On anatomical and physiological grounds, it is quite certain that these exercises are admirably calculated to liberate the ligaments of the fingers, and to give a freer play and increased vigour to those muscles upon which many of the varied and more independent movements of the fingers depend.

"I have no doubt whatever that such exercises will be of the greatest service in educating the fingers of musicians, and thereby save them a great deal of time and trouble"

From RICHARD QUAIN, F.R.S., *Professor of Clinical Surgery in University College; Surgeon Extraordinary to the Queen.*

Aug. 2nd, 1865.

"I write to you upon the important facts you were good enough to communicate to me to-day, and to explain how they may be accounted for scientifically. Your proposal to exercise the hand and fingers, and your plan of systematically carrying out the proposal so as to be beneficial to musicians, are *both new* to me. Judging on principle, and from a knowledge of what occurs in other parts of the body, I have no doubt that the system must be useful, for it will give increased mobility to the fingers and increased development and power to the small muscles—Lumbricales (the *musculi fidicinales* of Cowper), and metacarpal interosseous, as well as, indeed, to the general flexors and extensors of the hand. In short, the exercises you propose will be to the hand and fingers what the ordinary gymnastic exercises are to the rest of the limbs. The result will be useful wherever the free play and vigour of the fingers are needed; would therefore, I anticipate, be especially advantageous to musicians, and, I am inclined to add, to painters and to writers also." . . .

From ERASMUS WILSON, F.R.S.

"On carefully thinking over your demonstration of gymnastic exercises as applied to the hand, I can see in it only good; it is ingenious, practical, and physiological, and eminently adapted for the purpose to which you propose to adopt it; namely, the manipulation of the strings and keys of musical instruments. I am glad to hear that you intend to give your labours to the public very shortly. . . . I see no possible inconvenience, much less danger, in the process."

From DR. VIRCHOW, *Professor of Pathological Anatomy, Berlin.*

TRANSLATION. *June 3rd.*

•The exposition of your proposed Gymnastics for the regular exercise of those portions of the body which are used most partially, namely, the fingers, deserves, assuredly, a great and practical recogniton. They are addressed, according to my opinion, to a real want or hiatus. Not only will they very naturally serve as a special preparation for musical objects, but also for a like participation of the muscle-groups of the fore-arm and the hand, which, in all the usual labours of daily life, are only very partially brought into action. In the case of men who only write, and women who sew, or do other fine work, the great disadvantages arising from the special pressure in individual groups of muscles will be altogether avoided; and I regard it as extremely probable that your gymnastics will diminish or entirely remove many dis-orders, such as writing-cramp, contortions," &c.

Official extract from the books of the SOCIETY OF PHYSICIANS AT BERLIN *of the Meeting held by them, June 6th.*

President--DR. BEREND, Member of the Royal Privy Council, and Director of the Gymnastic-orthopedic Institution, Berlin.

Secretary—DR. GUMBINNER.

"Mr. Jackson, from England, delivered a lecture, in the German language, upon gymnastics of the fingers and wrist. The fatigue which immediately attended the playing on the violin late in life, incident even to a person strong and athletic in all other respects, led him to the discovery, after lengthened investigations, *first*, that the fingers are the least exercised of all the active muscles of the human body: *secondly*, that they are thereby, on physiological grounds, also the weakest; and *thirdly*, as he afterwards on minute investigation found out, that the finger-muscles are almost the only active muscles in the frame to which a properly consti-tuted system of gymnastics had never been applied.

"He discovered that the cause of this fatigue lies in the want of finger-training; and the lecturer explained, and adduced proof, that the muscles, hitherto constrained in their movements by tight transverse ligaments, are instantaneously set free by gymnastic stretching applica-tions to those ligaments. The society expressed itself entirely in accord with the theory as well as the practice which the lecturer adduced; they desired to add that both the one and the other are entirely new to them, and to express a belief that the same will be introduced into every school in Germany as soon as they shall be made known.

"In expressing their best thanks to Mr. Jackson for his most interesting discourse, the society desire to record the fact, which the lecturer in soliciting their indulgence stated, that he had commenced the study of the German language for the first time at a late period in life, namely, at the age of 52 years, exactly six years ago; nevertheless the lecturer seems to have mastered its great difficulties, and has delivered gratuitously this and many other lectures extempore in excellent German, an achievement which the society believes to be without precedent."

Expressions of marked approval have also been received from Sir W. FERGUSON, F.R.S., *Surgeon-Extraordinary to the Queen*, Professor R. OWEN, F.R.S., D.C.L., *British Museum*, Dr. JOSEHH HIRTH, *Professor of Anatomy, Vienna*, and other distinguished persons.

From JOHN HULLAH, *Professor of Music in King's College and in Queen's College; Organist of Charterhouse, &c.*
July 27th, 1865.

"Mr. Edwin W. Jackson has called attention to an anatomical fact which is likely to prove of great importance to students of instrumental music; and the apparatus and course of exercises by which he proposes to turn the knowledge of this fact to account seem well calculated for the attainment of the object he has in view—that of increasing the strength, pliability, and expansiveness of the hand."

From E. F. RIMBAULT, LL.D., F.S.A., *Member of the Royal Academy of Music in Stockholm; Musical Examiner in the Royal College of Preceptors, London &c, &c.*

'Mr. E. Ward-Jackson's discovery is of the *highest importance* to all performers on musical instruments requiring the use of the fingers. Several attempts have been made, at different times, to construct apparatus which would give strength and elasticity to these importa.: t members of the band; but they have all signally failed. Mr. Jackson has been the *first* to consider the subject *philosophically* and *anatomically.* His discovery will form an era in the progress of the manipulation of the art."

From SIR JULIUS BENEDICT, *Pianist.*
July 22nd, 1865.

"I believe that Mr. Jackson's simple but ingenious contrivance will be highly beneficial for the musical student, and contribute to the clearness of touch and independence of the fingers. Experiments on a large scale, and in schools where music is taught, would still more contribute to acquaint the public with his clevei and useful invention."

From PROFESSOR WYLDE, *Mus. Doc., Cantab.; Professor of Music in Gresham College.*
July 23rd, 1865.

"Many thanks for sending me your pamphlet, which I have read very carefully. It has interested me very much, and I have no doubt of the practical excellence of your discovery."

From PROSPER SAINTON, *Leader of the Royal Italian Opera, of the Sacred Harmonic Society; of the Musical Society of London; and of the New Philharmonic Society*
Aug. 5th, 1865.

"I have great pleasure in adding my testimony to that given to you by so many artists. I congratulate you upon your invention, which I am certain will be of great utility to pupils of the violin, in giving to their fingers strength and elasticity."

From WALTER MACFARREN, *Professor of the Pianoforte in the Royal Academy of Music.*
July 28th, 1865.

"Mr. Edwin W. Jackson has done me the favour to explain to me his new system of gymnastics for the fingers, and I have no hesitation in stating that, in my opinion, it is calculated to obtain, by the simplest means, the independence of wrist and flexibility of finger essential to the pianist, or indeed to the performer on any keyed instrument. I consider that the introduction of this system would be of great value to both professor and pupil in schools and conservatories where music is studied.

From Jos. JOACHIM, *Violinist*.

"I must, on reflection, admit that the gymnastics for the fingers which you suggest must, by proper application of the same, contribute greatly to strengthen and render pliant the finger-joints."

From PROFESSOR MOSCHELES.

"Your very ingenious discovery, that the necessary strength and flexibility of the fingers for pianoforte and violin playing can be effected by means of cylinders placed between the fingers and other appliances, must prove to be of great use."

From DR. H. H. PIERSON, *Professor of Music, Edinburgh*.

"Many thanks for your staff, which is an excellent idea, and a very useful invention, as well as the cylinders. The advice contained in your 'Finger und Handgelenk Gymnastik,' together with the set of regulations there laid down, is of eminent value, if properly attended to, as a means of preparing the fingers and wrist for playing the piano, violin, &c., and for rendering, them strong and flexible, the two indispensable requisites. I particularly admire the extreme simplicity of all your inventions, which really remind one of the 'Egg of Columbus,' and I should not be surprised if your ideas (so disinterestedly offered to the public) were to introduce a new era in the study of the pianoforte and stringed instruments. They must also be of signal service to organists, to whom I should specially recommend your apparatus."

From HENRY BLAGROVE, *Professor of the Royal Academy of Music; Leader of the Philharmonic Society; of the Musical Society of London, &c., &c.*

July 22nd, 1865.

"On perusal of your MS. relative to the development of the muscles of the hands, &c., as applied to musicians, I have great pleasure in offering you my testimony to its being a valuable adjunct to musical tuition where mechanical action is required, such as for the piano, or violin and violoncello. I think it shortens the usual routine of practising to gain strength, and will give at once freedom and force to the hand, fingers, arm," &c.

From J. T. CARRODUS, *Leader of Her Majesty's Theatre.*

July 23rd, 1865.

"I am convinced that Mr. Jackson's invention for the development of the muscles of the fingers and hand will be of great value to musical students."

From E. AGUILAR, *Pianist.*

July 22nd, 1865.

"I consider Mr. Ward-Jackson's system for the fingers remarkable for its simplicity, ingenuity, and efficacy. I believe that its universal adoption must materially benefit and assist all who cultivate instrumental music."

From W. GEO. CUSINS, *Pianist, Organist to Her Majesty.*

July 27th, 1865.

"I beg you will permit me to say how much interested I was this morning with the highly ingenious method of developing the hand you were kind enough to explain to me. I believe your discovery to be of great importance to musicians who use their fingers. For myself I intend trying your system, and shall likewise make my pupils use it."

From B. MOLIQUE, *Violinist.*

July 22nd, ₁ ;65.

"Mr. Jackson's gymnastic invention for the fingers and wrist will be of great benefit to musical students."

From J. BALSR CHATTERTON, *Harpist to Her Majesty the Queen.*

July 31th, 1865.

"I have taken time to think over your ingenious invention, and am of opinion that it will be of incalculable service to harp players. I can only hope that it will become extensively known, and shall be glad to hear of the publication of your forthcoming work."

From JOHN THOMAS, *Harpist, Professor of the Royal Academy of Music; Pencerdd Gwalia.*

July 25th, 1865.

"I have much pleasure in bearing testimony to the importance of Mr. Jackson's simple but clever invention for rendering the fingers independent of each other, and in preparing them for execution upon any musical instrument, thus greatly facilitating the attainment of execution; and I sincerely hope that his invention will be made public, in order that the world may derive the full benefit of it."

From LINDSAY SLOPER, *Pianist.*

July 31st, 1865.

"Allow me to express to you the interest I felt in your system of finger-gymnastics as shown to me by you last week. Your inventions seem to me very likely to produce the results you have sought, and I should be very glad to see their utility tested in our music-schools."

---

www.ingramcontent.com/pod-product-compliance
Lightning Source LLC
Chambersburg PA
CBHW021522270326

41930CB00008B/1042